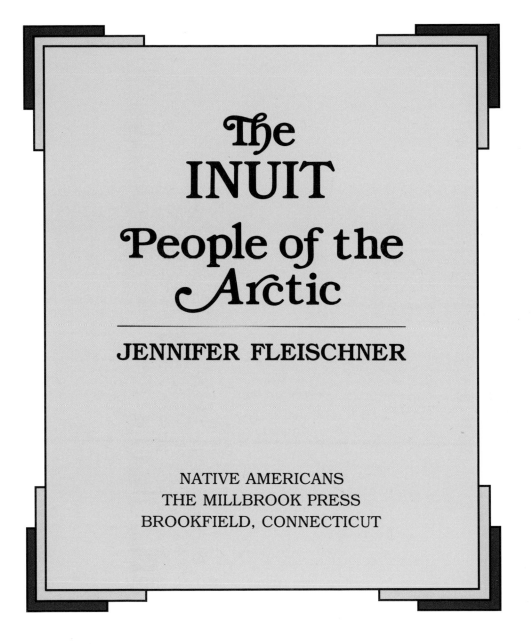

The
INUIT
People of the Arctic

JENNIFER FLEISCHNER

NATIVE AMERICANS
THE MILLBROOK PRESS
BROOKFIELD, CONNECTICUT

Cover: *Eskimo Wolf Dance #1* by Kivetoruk Moses, courtesy of the Anchorage Museum of History and Art.

Photographs courtesy of the New York Public Library Picture Collection: pp. 11, 18; Native American Painting Reference Library: p. 13; Werner Forman Archive, Haffenreffer Museum of Anthropology, Brown University, Rhode Island/Art Resource: p. 15; Magnum Photos: pp. 20 (© Rene Burri), 28 (© Burt Glinn), 30 (© Burt Glinn) 33 (© Arthur Tress); Art Resource: p. 23 (top: Scala, bottom: Aldo Tutino); Archives, Alaska and Polar Regions Department, University of Alaska, Fairbanks: pp. 25 (Lomen Collection, acc. #72-71-858N), 41 (Romig Collection, acc. #90-043-200N), 43 (Lomen Collection, acc. #72-71-826), 50 (VF-Eskimos with Reindeer-Sleds, acc. #62-2036-195); Photo Researchers: p. 26 (Phyllis McCutcheon); Werner Forman/Art Resource: p. 35; North Wind Picture Archives: pp. 37, 47; Hudson's Bay Company Archives, Provincial Archives of Manitoba: p. 40; First Light, Toronto: p. 53 (© Robert Semeniuk). Map by Joe LeMonnier.

Library of Congress Cataloging-in-Publication Data
Fleischner, Jennifer.
The Inuit : people of the Arctic / by Jennifer Fleischner.
p.   cm. — (Native Americans)
Includes bibliographical references (p.   ) and index.
Summary: The history and culture of the Inuit,
whose ancestors crossed the Bering Strait to Alaska
around 3000 B.C. Includes an Inuit craft and game.
ISBN 1-56294-587-4 (Lib. Bdg.)
1. Inuit—History—Juvenile literature.   2. Inuit—Social life and customs—Juvenile literature.   [1. Inuit.   2. Eskimos.]   I. Title.
II. Series.
E99.E7F56   1995   979.8'004971—dc20   94-42235   CIP   AC

CONTENTS

The Inuit

INUIT LANDS

FACTS ABOUT THE TRADITIONAL INUIT WAY OF LIFE

GROUP NAME:
Inuit, meaning "the people"

MAJOR DIVISIONS:
Alaskan Eskimo, Central Eskimo, and Greenland
(Polar) Eskimo (Aleut closely related)

GEOGRAPHIC REGION:
Northeast Siberia, western and northern Alaska, northern
Canada, western and eastern coasts of Greenland, and
northern Labrador (Aleut on Aleutian Islands off Alaska)

LANGUAGE:
Eskimo-Aleut

HOUSE TYPE:
Snow igloos, wooden houses, stone-and-turf houses,
semi-underground wood-and-sod houses

MAIN FOODS:
Game (caribou, bears, hares, seals, whales); fish (salmon,
Arctic char, lake trout, cod); and birds

A FROZEN LAND

It was early December 1850 when two Inuit hunters stood silently on the sea ice on the northern coast of Alaska, several miles from shore. They were peering intently across the frozen surface at a small hole a few feet away. It was hard to see. The temperature was 15 degrees below zero Fahrenheit (−26°C), and in the bitter cold a mist of steam, like a fluffy cloud, blew back and forth over the surface of the ice. The sun never rose at that time of year, but at midday a glowing orange light pushed up above the southern horizon, giving the men a few hours of pale light for hunting.

The journey across the sea ice had been treacherous. Most of the ice had turned from gray to white, which meant that it was now thick enough to support a man and his loaded dogsled. But irregular freezing and thawing and a heavy wind had made cracks and weak spots where an unwary hunter could fall through. Cracks were also hidden beneath windblown snow. Luckily, the hunters' dogs often shied away from the thin spots, where the watery ice chilled their paws. But the safest way to judge thickness was by jabbing an ice-hunting harpoon, called an *unaak*, into the ice. This was a pole with an iron spike at one end and a hook at the other, and every experienced Inuit hunter carried one.

The hunters were watching at a breathing hole, or *aglu*, of the ringed seal. They knew that this *aglu* was being used by several seals, and they hoped to be able to kill two or three before the day was over. Seals make their breathing holes when the ice is just forming and still thin enough to break through. As the ice thickens, the seals must keep the holes big enough for their heads to fit through. They will gnaw and scratch through the ice to keep their holes from freezing over.

Winter sealing meant long waits in intense cold and piercing wind. Dressing properly for the cold could be the difference between life and death. Both men wore sealskin boots, called *kamiks*, which reached up to their knees. They had on white bearskin trousers and coats of fox fur with long hoods that were pulled forward over their ears. The fur was on the inside, because this made the coats warmer. Beneath their coats, the men wore waterproof shirts made of strips of walrus intestine sewn together. It was important to stay as dry as possible. If an Inuit hunter's clothes became wet, and he took them off to dry, he might not be able to put them on again since they would be frozen stiff.

An hour passed. The younger man pulled one hand out of his caribou mitten and held it briefly over his face to warm the skin. He stamped his feet often to keep from feeling the cold. The older Inuit sat down on a small block of ice, resting his feet on a strip of fur. His harpoon lay on his right, its line coiled in his lap.

An Inuit hunter, harpoon at the ready, waits motionlessly at the breathing hole of a seal. The huge ice wedges of the tundra loom in the background.

Suddenly, the older hunter tilted his head to the ice. The younger man stopped moving. There was the slightest bubbling and spray in the breathing hole, then the sound of scratching. Soon, both men heard the breathing of a seal—first a short breath, to smell the air and check for danger, then a deep and long breath. In one motion, the older hunter stood up, raised his harpoon, aimed, and struck. The younger man worked quickly to widen the hole, and together they pulled the seal onto the ice.

THE ARCTIC NORTH ▪ Of all the many peoples in the world, only the Inuit have made the Arctic their permanent home. This is the area in North America that lies closest to the North Pole, and for roughly five thousand years, the Inuit have lived in these northernmost regions of the earth. It is a treeless landscape where the temperature in the summer does not rise above 50°F (10°C). There the ground remains frozen all year round, except under large bodies of water, and hard winds blow the snow around. The land is called *tundra*. Ice wedges rise out of the snow-covered ground, as tall as one-story buildings. Ice-covered hills and mountains loom up over the white expanse. The landscape has a hypnotic sameness as far as the eye can see. Between November and March there is darkness twenty-four hours a day, but between May and September the sun never sets. It is a severe land, yet also one of unimaginable beauty.

Over the centuries, the Inuit developed a way of life that enabled them to survive in this harsh environment. Because they have lived where nobody else has wanted to, they have kept more of their traditions and territories than other native peoples, who had to fight with outsiders over their ancient lands. For instance, although most modern-day Inuit hunters no longer use harpoons, favoring the more effective rifle, many of the techniques of breathing-hole hunting have been the same for centuries. Because they were so isolated many Inuit were relatively undisturbed by outside influences. This helps to explain the remarkable unity of culture that ties together the different Inuit groups, who are scattered all across the north, reaching from the northeast coast of Siberia, western and northern Alaska, and across Canada, to eastern Greenland. A closely related Arctic people, the Aleut, live on the Aleutian Islands, which are off the Alaska Peninsula.

HOW THEY CAME ▪ The Inuit ancestors came to North America from Siberia around 3000 B.C., probably crossing the Bering Strait between Siberia and Alaska in skin or wooden boats, or by riding the ice floes. Like the Asian peoples from whom they are descended, the Inuit are generally a short, broad people, with round faces, light-brown skin, and the epicanthic eye fold, which is the small fold of skin over the inner corner of the eye.

At a winter camp, a hunter guts his kill and hangs the raw meat on a rail to dry. It took many hundreds of pounds of meat to feed a camp through the harsh winter.

Inuit, which simply means "the people," is the name the Inuit call themselves, although for years Europeans knew them as "Eskimos," an Algonquian name meaning "eaters of raw meat." Traditionally, the Inuit survived mostly by hunting caribou, seals, bears, wolves, hares, foxes, musk oxen, whales, and many kinds of birds. They fished for salmon, trout, Arctic char, and cod. They lived a semi-nomadic existence, moving as the seasons changed. Camps were made up of several families loosely grouped together. Because survival was harder during the winter, winter camps would require more people than summer camps, and might have close to one hundred people, while summer hunting groups could have fewer than twelve.

THE EARLIEST INUIT ▪ The Inuit prehistory (before written records) is divided into three cultures: Pre-Dorset, Dorset, and Thule. The Pre-Dorset culture began when Inuit ancestors from Siberia arrived in Alaska some three thousand years ago. These ancient people used small blades of flint to cut bone and ivory into harpoons and lances. To cut meat and skin, they fashioned handles out of antlers and set the blades in them. They probably made skin-covered boats. Their oval houses were partially sunk in the ground for warmth, and most likely were covered with skin.

Between 700 and 500 B.C., during a period of warmer temperatures, the Dorset culture evolved. Some early examples of Inuit art date to this period. The Dorsets shaped harpoon heads to look like bears and falcons and used them in religious and magical ceremonies. They carved masks, human figures, and animal, fish, and bird images out of ivory, bone, antlers, and sometimes wood.

This comb is an artifact of the Dorset period. The carving shows an archer aiming at some animals. (Early Inuit brought the bow and arrow with them from Asia, and may have been responsible for introducing this weapon to North America.)

Beginning around A.D. 1000, the Thule culture developed and spread out across the entire Arctic. They were whaling people, who hunted the great bowhead and baleen whales. The Thules devised the tools and survival techniques that the later Inuit used. They sharpened harpoons and darts to hunt whales, walruses, and seals. They sat on three-legged stools alongside breathing holes of the ringed seal, equipped with harpoons, ice picks, and scoops. They shot land animals with bows and arrows made of sinew and bone and fished with spears.

Thule hunters also knew how to train dogs to haul their loaded sleighs or carry packs. And they paddled on the sea in kayaks and *umiaks* (open skin boats used in whale hunting). They also built sturdy winter houses out of whalebone, earth, and flat stones. The roofs were held up with whale-jaw rafters.

The Thules made more than just hunting tools for men. They carved delicate combs, thimble holders, needle cases, and pendants for Thule women to use. They also created beautiful "swimming figurines." These small carved figures were of the upper part of the female body — the rest, it was understood, was beneath an imaginary waterline. They were worn as amulets, magical charms against evil or disease.

THE "LITTLE ICE AGE" ▪ Beginning about A.D. 1200, temperatures began to fall. Between 1400 and 1500, a "Little Ice Age" of very cold temperatures set in. During this time, the sea ice never melted and whales could not migrate into Thule hunting grounds. As a result, the Thules came to rely more heavily on summer hunting of land mammals and on caribou and seals in the winter.

By 1700, Thule culture had become what we know of as Inuit culture. Changes were sweeping across the Arctic: European explorers and fur traders had arrived, seeking wealth and adventure in the frozen land.

"THE PEOPLE"

The Inuit are divided into three major cultural groups: the Alaskan Eskimo, the Central Eskimo, and the Greenland (Polar) Eskimo. Along with the Aleut, the Inuit share the same language family, called Eskimo-Aleut, although many dialects are spoken by the various Inuit groups. For the Inuit and Aleut, everyday life has always consisted of doing the chores necessary for survival in the Arctic. Over the centuries, the Inuit and Aleut devised a way of life that made it possible to live in the bitterest cold weather.

INUIT HOUSES ▪ To survive in the frigid Arctic, the Inuit of the seventeenth and eighteenth centuries had to be able to build houses out of the materials at hand: snow, animal skins and bones, earth, stones, wood, and driftwood. An Inuit could live for days without food, but without proper shelter death would come in hours. An Inuit hunter caught by a blizzard far from home knew how to turn a sleigh upside down, pack snow around it, and sleep under it. This temporary shelter would keep him warm for the night.

The Inuit built different kinds of shelters, depending on where they lived. Where there were forests, as in southern Alaska, the Inuit had above-ground wooden houses. Other Alaskan Eskimos constructed wood-and-sod houses that were partially underground. Greenland Eskimos lived in houses made of stone and turf, with waterproof gut-skin windows. The Aleuts lived in pit houses built of timber with dirt and sod packed around the structure.

The typical winter dwelling of the northernmost Inuit (such as the Polar Eskimos in Greenland) was the *igluviak*,

A village made up of many igluviaks, bustling with activity after a successful hunt.

which means "snowhouse." (Most people call them *igloos*, but to the Inuit, all houses are igloos.) Igluviaks were built from the ground up out of "bricks" of tightly packed tundra snow, which provided insulation against the cold. The whole family would help in the construction. After the men sketched a circle into the snow as a base, cut the wedge-shaped blocks and piled them up, the women and children would pack snow between the blocks and throw snow over the whole house.

The rounded walls curved up and inward, about 9 feet (almost 3 meters) from the floor to the center of the ceiling, and 15 feet (almost 5 meters) in diameter. The dome shape of the igluviaks prevented them from being blown over by the strong Arctic winds: In fact, the winds would pack the snow even tighter, making the houses stronger over time. An entrance tunnel kept out the colder outside air. A skin covered the entrance hole, which could then be closed for the night with a block of snow. The tunnel also served to give warning to the family that visitors had arrived. Guests would stand in the entry tunnel and call out, while using a *tilugtut*, a small saber of wood or bone, to beat the snow crystals off their clothes. Otherwise, the snow would melt as soon as they entered, making clothes uncomfortably wet and heavy.

Since warm air rises, the warmest part of the igluviak was closest to the dome. So the Inuit built platforms off the ground for cooking, working, playing, and sleeping. The family slept together all in a row beneath blankets of fox, hare, caribou, and duck skins.

Heated by a little soapstone lamp that burned blubber for fuel, the igluviak was warm enough for the family to be able to

Dogsleds proved to be the most efficient way to cross the ice and snow of the tundra plains.

remove their heaviest clothes. Light filtered through the walls of snow, but sometimes windows were cut above the entrance tunnel. These cutouts were fitted with windowpanes of seal intestines.

INUIT LIFE ▪ Inuit life was shaped completely by the demands of the extreme Arctic conditions. The men's days were occupied by hunting and fishing. Before the nineteenth century, when rifles exchanged in the fur trade gained widespread use, hunters used harpoons, lances, knives, and spears to hunt.

The dogsled was the main means of travel for hunting or moving the family from one camp to another. A team of ten dogs could pull a sleigh carrying 800 pounds (360 kilograms) or more.

Hunters killed whales and seals, leaning out from kayaks and umiaks on the open sea. Hunters had to be able to throw their harpoons more than 20 feet (6 meters), or pull in a struggling walrus weighing 2,000 pounds (about 900 kilograms). High winds and rough water made this form of hunting dangerous, and women would often climb neighboring hills to watch for their husbands to return at the end of the day. A hunter rarely hunted alone, and all those who participated in the kill would share the meat. The hunter who struck the animal first ("first harpoon") got the best parts, however.

HUNTING RITUALS ▪ The Inuit believed that spirits lived in all natural things. The Sea Mother lived in land and sea animals. The Raven Father was associated with thunder, lightning, and storms. Hunters would seek the help of these spirits with prayers and offerings of fish. Charms in the shape of ravens were thought to be powerful forces contributing to success in the hunt. Whale hunts often resembled religious ceremonies with their own ritual poems:

The north wind is a man.
The north wind keeps the sea ice open
for the whales to swim through.

The south wind is a woman.
When the south wind blows, the sea ice closes.
Then hunters come in and wait for open water.

MAKING CLOTHING ▪ While the men hunted, the women's daily chore was to make and repair clothes from the skins and furs. This important task required great skill and patience. The women would spend much of their day cutting the animal skins and stitching them together. A woman would sit in her igluviak with her legs stretched out and her work on the floor between them. With her *ulo*, a crescent-shaped bone knife, she scraped and cut the skins without measuring them, then chewed and rubbed them until they were soft. Next she stitched the pieces together invisibly with strong thread made from caribou sinew. Needles made of ivory or the hard wing or leg of a bird were prized possessions and were kept in small, intricately decorated tubes. Just as a man's skill as a hunter made him desirable as a husband, so a woman's talent for sewing was one of her great attractions as a wife. An Arctic traveler could not afford to have a tear in his bearskin trousers or caribou fur coat, since either could mean death by freezing.

To keep warm, the Inuit tailored specialized clothing, which featured many layers of different materials. Air trapped between the layers insulated the body from the cold. Men, women, and children wore basically the same clothing: waterproof sealskin boots called *kamiks*; white bearskin pants; a seal, caribou, or fox fur coat; caribou or sealskin mittens; and bird-skin shirts. They sewed their parkas to hang loosely and in double layers over the body, but to fit snugly at the neck and wrists, and they lined their boots and mittens with down and moss. The women's kamiks were longer than the men's, reaching to the top of the thigh, and their larger hoods were edged with foxtails. They carried their babies in *amauts*, pouches that

Right: A flask-shaped storage case for sewing needles. Below: A parka made of seal or walrus intestines.

were sewn inside the back of their coats. When indoors, the Inuit took off most of their clothing. This was thought to be a good way to "air" the body. A rubdown with a little whale oil was also considered to be cleansing.

Like other northern Indians, the Inuit decorated their faces and bodies with tattoos. A bone needle, threaded with sinew or hair dipped in lampblack or plant juice, was pulled through the skin. Tattoo marks were also made by pricking holes into the flesh with a sharp bone. The women's faces were decorated with lines that radiated from the mouth over the cheeks, chin, and forehead. Men sometimes wore ivory labrets, ornaments that hung from the corners of the mouth or under the lower lip.

"MEAT AND MEAT, AND MEAT AGAIN" ▪ Visiting and feasting were central to the community life of the Inuit. The isolated life of the Arctic might explain why the Inuit delighted in visiting. Families who were constantly moving from one hunting ground to another might not see relatives or friends for months on end. It was customary to hold feasts whenever plenty of food was available, since game could become scarce at any time.

Not surprisingly, the Inuit placed a high value on hospitality. It was a point of pride to serve guests the best pieces of meat in the house. A hunter who had a successful catch was a happy man, for he could invite his neighbors to join him in a feast. After his guests arrived, the hunter went to the meat rack outside to bring in his prize. He would apologize for how sorry a piece of meat it was, even though he was actually very pleased with it. Then his guests would help him lug the huge bulk in through the entrance tunnel while groaning about how heavy it was and how great a hunter their host was.

*This photograph of a young Inuit woman
shows the tattoos on her chin.*

Peter Freuchen, a Danish traveler who, starting in 1906, lived among the Inuit on and off for forty years, recounted how he learned which portions of an animal were good to eat. "When you have meat and meat, and meat again," he wrote, "you learn to distinguish between the different parts. . . ." Among the Polar Inuit with whom Freuchen lived, *narwhal* (spotted whale) skin was a great delicacy. This was eaten fresh or raw or preserved for later use in bags of dried meat and blubber. Fish and blood soup were also relished. But the most festive treat was a *giviak*, which means "something dipped." Freuchen describes feasting

Ice fishing required long hours of patience and stamina. The reward for the hunter was being able to proudly invite his neighbors for a feast.

on a giviak made of auks (the auk is a small bird) that had been immersed in seal blubber and ripened over the course of the summer. Because it was winter at the time of this feast, the host had to chip away at the frozen giviak with an ax, which sent feathers and bird meat flying in all directions.

In general, meat was eaten boiled, dried, or raw. Guests would pass around the meat, cutting off hunks of it for themselves. Water melted from snow was shared from a basin of walrus skin or sealskin. A feast might last for hours, with guests falling asleep where they sat, and waking up later to pick up the meal where they left off.

Food and gifts were also exchanged during ritual "asking feasts," which were formal methods of trading. A prosperous hunter might host a feast for his equal from another community, and the feast would be followed by an exchange of goods. Inland caribou hunters might trade furs and skins for the seal oil, whalebone, and ivory that seal hunters had.

Given their diet of "meat and meat," it may seem surprising that the Inuit did not suffer from scurvy, an illness caused by lack of vitamin C. But the raw skin of a white whale or narwhal has as much vitamin C as oranges. And raw liver, another Inuit food, is rich in vitamins A and D.

FAMILIES ▪ Parents, children, aunts, uncles, and grandparents lived in one shelter, or in several close by. Orphans or relatives who had no hunters to provide for them were also taken into the Inuit family. An old person who believed himself to be a burden might voluntarily stay behind to die when the family moved on.

Inuit families had to work hard together just to survive. This photograph shows a contemporary Inuit family pulling their sled up to their shelter. They probably have been out gathering firewood.

Marriages took place as soon as a man could provide enough food for a wife and after a woman had reached puberty. There were no fixed rules about courtship. Sometimes young people were promised to one another at birth. Other times a man visited his chosen's family to ask the approval of her father. In some cases, however, a hunter would simply decide to take a woman from her home and begin living with her. Successful hunters might have more than one wife to do all the work that had to be done. Wife exchanges among hunters were also common. If a hunter was going on a long trip and for some reason his wife could not travel, he might ask to "borrow" a neighbor's wife for the journey. This was one way to form a partnership between the hunters. It was considered rude for a man to refuse to "lend" his wife. Women had little or no say in these matters.

Because so many chores had to be done to survive, children, especially sons, were valued. The Inuit treated their children with great care; in fact, it was the opinion of many European visitors that the Inuit spoiled their children. Children were allowed to play freely wherever they wanted and were rarely scolded. The Inuit felt that it was a joy to watch children's careless play, since wisdom and good sense would come naturally with adulthood.

Baby boys were expected to grow up to be fine hunters. When a boy was about eight, he would begin learning how to build a snowhouse or to track game and make weapons. A boy's first caribou or seal kill was celebrated with a small feast. Girls were taught how to set traps, how to trim the wick of the *kudlik*, or stone lamp, and how to make and mend clothes. Their mothers passed down their knowledge of patterns and stitches to their young daughters. Both boys and girls learned how to handle dogs and drive a sled.

GAMES ▪ Because of the severe climate, Inuit families spent hours indoors playing games and telling stories. Gambling games were especially popular. In one game, one side guessed who on the other side was holding certain carved bones under a cover. In another, players dropped pieces of seal flipper bones

Cat's Cradle String Game

The Inuit were fond of string games, in which they would use their fingers to shape figures out of a circle of sinew thread. Inuit women were especially good at this, and spent many hours inventing complicated patterns.

The following string game is played by one person, but with a partner the game can go on and on, from the simple "cat's cradle" to the more complicated "soldier's bed" and "candles."

Start by looping the string around the fingers of both hands. Leave your thumbs out of the loop.

Now loop it around both hands once more so that it wraps around the back of your hands twice and crosses your palms once.

Reach across with the middle finger of your right hand and catch the string that runs across your left palm. Pull your hands apart.

Do the same thing with your left middle finger. Reach across and hook under the string that crosses your right hand. Pull your hands apart. Look down: It's a cat's cradle.

carved in the shapes of animals or people onto a fur mat; the player with the most pieces standing upright would win. String games such as cat's cradle were common. The Inuit also played a game in which players tried to stick a long needle into holes that had been drilled into a bone hanging from above. Outdoor games were tests of physical skill, such as running, tug-of-war, rock throwing, or wrestling.

STORYTELLING ▪ Among some Inuit, social life was centered in a *kashim*, or big snowhouse. The community would gather here to dance, sing, feast, tell stories, or hold religious ceremonies. (The Inuit have an oral culture, which means that they remember and preserve their past through stories, poems, and songs that they pass down through the spoken word from generation to generation.) They sang about nature and the spirit world that they believed lived in all nature. One of the most famous Arctic travelers, Knud Rasmussen, translated and wrote down this Inuit poem in the early 1920s:

> *Glorious it is to see*
> *The caribou flocking down from the forests*
> *And beginning*
> *Their wandering to the north.*
> *Timidly they watch*
> *For the pitfalls of man.*
> *Glorious it is to see*
> *The great herds from the forests*
> *Spreading out over plains of white.*
> *Glorious to see.*

The Inuit, like people everywhere, used stories to teach values, explain the mysteries of the world, and just pass the time. One of the oldest tales is about "the girl who didn't want a husband." Instead, her father makes her marry a handsome stranger who is really a dog. When she is ready to give birth, her father puts her alone on an island, where she has a litter of children, half of them dogs and half of them human. The human children become the ancestors of the Inuit, while the dogs become the ancestors of the "whites" and the Indians. Later, she changes into the Sea Mother, who lives at the bottom of the sea and controls all the animals on land and sea. Other popular Inuit stories told about the brother and sister who became the moon and the sun, or about the orphan boy who grew up to become a great hero to his people.

THE SPIRIT WORLD ▪ Certain Inuit men and women were considered to be shamans, or *angakoks*, people with supernatural powers who could cure and cause disease, control the weather, and find lost people. Angakoks usually acquired their power through long periods of fasting and isolation. During certain rituals, angakoks put themselves in touch with the spirit world.

Among the Inuit, the soul was viewed as a miniature image of the person and it lived inside the body. The Inuit believed that when a person died, the soul was reborn in a newborn infant. So when a baby was born, he or she would be named after a relative who had recently died. People with the same name were therefore thought to share a soul relationship. If the soul fell ill or died, the body would too. Loss of the soul was believed to cause illness, and angakoks cured the sick by re-

An angakok (shaman) with a drum made of seal-skin intestines. In the background are arches made of whalebones, used during many ceremonies.

storing the soul to the body. The Inuit also believed the soul lived on after a person's death, and angakoks would conduct ceremonies during which they would be taken over by the dead person's soul. Angakoks were also said to be able to leave their own bodies and take the shapes of different animals.

The angakoks also made sure that their people obeyed certain *taboos*, the things or actions that were forbidden. Many of the taboos required the strict separation of anything having to do with land and sea animals. For instance, Inuit women were not allowed to sew caribou skins in snowhouses that were built on the sea ice during the months of darkness or while the men were hunting walruses. The Inuit also avoided eating the meat of land and sea animals in the same meal. Bad weather, sickness, or poor hunting were often blamed on the violation of a taboo. Angakoks would suggest ways of soothing the offended spirits with special gifts. They also set punishments for whoever broke the taboo.

SOCIAL ORDER ▪ The Inuit had no chiefs or headmen to set rules or punish wrongdoings. Instead, problems were handled through blood feuds. Anyone who felt badly treated was expected to take revenge against the wrongdoer and his entire family. The practice of blood feuds tended to discourage crime, since it put the whole group in danger. Another common way to deal with social problems was through public shaming and ridicule. Peter Freuchen tells of how an entire community decided to punish a man named Kayuk who was stealing seal liver from the group's meat rack. In order to punish Kayuk, another hunter replaced the seal liver with the liver of an old dog. All the villagers found excuses to watch Kayuk as he feasted on the dark meat. By the next morning he was terribly sick, to no one's surprise but his own.

Soap Carving

The Inuit are famous for their beautiful soapstone carvings of animal figures. To make a carving of your own, you will need a bar of white soap, a spoon, and a cloth. Begin by scraping off the name of the soap imprinted on the face of the bar. Then hold the bar in your hand and think about what animal shape you would like it to take. Inuit artists believed that there was a soul in all things and that their carving would release the soul's image. So before carving, an Inuit artist would feel the stone all over to try to understand the soul inside.

When you have decided what you want to carve, use the edge of the spoon to make slow, small cuts in the soap. Soon your animal shape will emerge. When you are finished, rub a damp cloth all over the soap sculpture to smooth it down.

*The Inuit also used ivory, as shown
here, for their animal carvings.*

EARLY
ENCOUNTERS

Norsemen settled in Greenland as early as the eleventh century. They began the centuries-long process of European influence on Inuit culture, especially on their economy and religion. Between the sixteenth and nineteenth centuries, explorers, traders, missionaries, whalers, and scientists arrived by ship from France, England, Scotland, Russia, and Scandinavia. The Inuit helped the Europeans, who often met disaster in the seemingly barren land. Explorers whose ships were wrecked on the icy cliffs were frozen in during winter or unable to find food.

The advance of Europeans into the Arctic was generally peaceful, since the Europeans knew they had to rely on the Inuit as guides and trappers, and the Inuit themselves were too spread out and few in number to threaten the newcomers. Stories claiming that groups of missing explorers were murdered by the Inuit trickled back to the settlements, but were usually proven false. "I don't doubt but what some of the said vessels' crews might be destroyed by the Esquemays," commented Moses Norton, governor in the late 1700s of Fort Churchill on Hudson Bay in present-day Manitoba, Canada.

"But . . . I have reason to believe that the Natives . . . would rather assist a man in distress than to do otherwise by him."

The earliest records of these European explorations convey the voyagers' amazement at Arctic living conditions. "This is the land God gave to Cain," wrote Jacques Cartier on arriving on the north shore of the Gulf of St. Lawrence in eastern Canada in 1534. "It is composed of stones and horrible rugged rock. . . . There is nothing but moss and short, stunted shrubs." Another

*The first European explorers in the Arctic made
their way through the treacherous, frozen
landscape, astonished that humans lived there.*

sixteenth-century explorer, George Best, who captained the Englishman Martin Frobisher's expedition to Baffin Island in northern Canada, was struck by the Inuit's method of getting food: "These people . . . hunte for their dinners . . . even as the Beare" (that is, just as bears do).

Sixteenth- and seventeenth-century voyagers often came seeking better trade routes between East Asia and Europe. Following in Henry Hudson's wake, explorers voyaged around the great Canadian inland sea of Hudson Bay in search of the mythical Northwest Passage. There, they discovered many natural ports and harbors, which were used by merchants and traders to open fur trade with the Inuit.

The treacherous northern climate kept away the huge numbers of Europeans who were competing for wealth in the more inviting southern territories of North America. The Inuit were aware that the arrival of Europeans had brought great changes to other native cultures in North America, and were sometimes grateful for their own isolation. In 1756, one Greenland Inuit made this address to his land: "How well it is that, if in your rocks there are gold and silver, for which the Christians are so greedy, it is covered with so much snow that they cannot get at it! Your unfruitfulness makes us happy and saves us from molestation!"

WHALERS ▪ But Europeans did find riches in the sea and land animals of the north. From the seventeenth through the early nineteenth centuries, hundreds of English, Scottish, and American whalers descended upon the Arctic shores. The Inuit's first contacts with these whaling ships were sometimes terrifying experiences. Angakoks would chant to ward off any possible evil that might come from the white strangers. Soon, however, the Inuit were hunting primarily for the European whalers, and not for their own families. The Inuit gave the whalers oil, blubber, whalebone, and furs. In return, they received flour, crackers, tobacco, tea, brandy, matches, lead, rifles, ammunition, and molasses.

In the nineteenth century, New England whalers dominated commercial whaling throughout the world. In the Arctic, they introduced a practice called *wintering*, meaning that whaling crews began spending winters living ashore in huts until the spring, when they went back to their ships. The Inuit would leave their winter camps and move to the land stations set up by the whalers. Living and working side by side, foreign whalers and the Inuit became dependent on each other, and their cultures blended together. Many whalers took Inuit women as temporary wives, and the children they had were raised as Inuit. To this day many Inuit are descended from such mixed backgrounds.

Words the Inuit had never needed now became part of their language. *Sailor* became *seealar*, meaning "a follower." *Flour* was called *puatigee*. European sailors, too lazy to learn the Inuit names, made up new ones. The names they invented for the native hunters, Wager Dick or John L. By 'n' By, are still sometimes used by the Inuit when they deal with Europeans, although they use their Inuit names at home.

TRADERS ▪ Europeans looked to the Arctic territories for the valuable furs that they fashioned into hats and clothes. In the

The Hudson's Bay Company, founded in Canada in 1670, set up trading posts to serve the fur traders, hunters, and merchants who came to trade in the Arctic.

eighteenth century, Russian fur hunters and traders established themselves in western Alaska. At first, the trade in fox, sea otter, and other furs was controlled by a few ambitious individual businessmen or small companies, who had outposts all along the Aleutian Islands off the coast of Alaska. Then, in 1781, Siberian merchants formed themselves into a larger company to enable them to extend their business to neighboring islands and the Alaskan mainland. By 1799, the Russian-American Company, under Aleksandr Baranov, had complete control over the fur trade in Alaska and the Aleutian Islands.

Meanwhile, in Labrador, German missionaries set up busy trading posts to support their missions. Their main goal was not to make money but to convert the Inuit to Christianity. After 1771, these priests received permission from the British government to build stations along the Labrador coast. Unlike other fur traders, the Germans did not trade brandy for the furs, but only practical goods, such as guns, ammunition, nails, twine, tea, and woolen clothing. They encouraged Inuit

German missionaries pose with the native population of a small village in Alaska. The missionaries spread out all across the Arctic, trading with the Inuit and teaching Christianity.

crafts, such as basket weaving and ivory carving, and introduced seal nets to the Inuit hunters. They also organized fisheries for salmon, cod, and char. By 1850, under the direction of the Germans, the Inuit were made to follow a yearly schedule for hunting. Fur trapping was done between Christmas and Easter; caribou hunting season was in April; seal hunting, May through July; fishing, July through September; and netting seals, from October through Christmas.

French and British fur traders alternated control over the Hudson Bay trade in the eighteenth and nineteenth centuries. French traders were masters of canoe travel, a skill they had learned from Indians. Beaver was the most important fur during this time, although mink, marten, wolverine, and weasel were also highly valued.

Overall, the Inuit's relations with the foreign fur traders were friendly. By the late eighteenth century, the Inuit had grown dependent on the goods they received from the Europeans, and they did not want to spoil their trading relationship. Stories of cheating on both sides were often treated casually, although occasional fights broke out. There was also a history of fighting between the Inuit and Indian groups in Alaska, which tended to flare up around trading posts. The Inuit blamed the Europeans for arming their Indian enemies with guns. Not long after the 1756 massacre of forty Inuit by a Cree war party, British traders taught the Inuit how to fire rifles.

As the fur trade expanded, the Inuit were important as guides and interpreters for the European explorers and traders. They also served as unofficial ambassadors of goodwill, smoothing rough encounters between the European outsiders

*By the mid-1700s the Inuit had, for the most part, given
up their harpoons in favor of rifles for hunting seals.*

and local Inuit. One of the most beloved and respected of the
Inuit guides was Tatanoyuk, or Augustus, as he was known to
the Europeans. Born about 1795 on Hudson Bay, he worked for
the Hudson's Bay Company as an interpreter for the Cree Indians and the British. Tatanoyuk died in 1834 when he was
separated from his companions during a storm.

Chapter Four

THE AGE OF CHANGE

The European explorers of the Arctic left their names on land and water across the north: Hudson Bay; Frobisher Bay; Baffin Island and Baffin Bay; Davis Strait; Mackenzie River; McClure Strait; Franklin Strait; Bering Strait. Whatever Inuit or Indian names these places may once have had are long forgotten. Nor do any of these places bear the names of the Inuit guides to whom many explorers owed their fame and, sometimes, their lives.

EXPLORATION IN WESTERN ALASKA ▪ During the eighteenth century, Russia's czar Peter the Great realized the importance of trade with northwestern America. To establish Russian outposts in Alaska, he ordered Vitus Bering, a Danish fleet captain in the Russian Navy, to lead an expedition to explore the coast of America. Bering set sail across the strait that now bears his name, but returned to Russia without ever sighting the American continent. Even though his expedition failed, it ignited interest in further exploration. In 1741, Bering embarked on his second expedition. This time, the expedition did reach the

American coast. They saw signs of human habitation but encountered no natives. Eventually, Bering's ship wrecked on Bering Island, where he and many crew members died during the winter.

In the early nineteenth century, Russian explorers, sponsored by the Russian government and the Russian-American Company, sought to spread the fur trade deeper into the Alaskan interior. As elsewhere, they encouraged the Alaskan Inuit to become dependent on the Russian-American Company for survival, at the expense of the Inuit's traditional self-sufficient way of life.

Meanwhile, beginning in the final decades of the eighteenth century, non-Russian expeditions into northwestern Alaska were led by such English navigators and explorers as Captain James Cook and Captain George Vancouver, who were beginning to map out the shape of Alaska that we know today. In contrast to the Russians, who were primarily motivated by the fur trade, these and other English and American explorers were mostly concerned with extending knowledge of the land itself. However, as time went on, and Russia and America began to compete for influence in Alaska, each country sought to extend its political power through exploration and expansion.

SIR JOHN FRANKLIN ▪ Several explorers penetrated deep into the central and northern Arctic during the first half of the nineteenth century. The most famous was Captain John Franklin. Between 1819 and 1845, when he vanished northwest of King William Island, Franklin led three expeditions along the

Arctic seaboard. For the first expedition in 1819 he recruited boatmen from the fur trade who could help him navigate the Coppermine River by canoe and map the Arctic shore going east as far as Hudson Bay. Without native guides, Franklin managed to mark down 550 miles (885 kilometers) of coastline before stopping. But he lost half of his men to cold and hunger on the overland journey back.

When he began his second journey in 1826, Franklin knew how to cope with the conditions of the Arctic. And this time, he had the services of the Inuit guide Tatanoyuk. It was Tatanoyuk who saved Franklin and his men when Franklin's party stumbled upon an encampment of armed Inuit who seemed ready to attack. Speaking in the dialect, Tatanoyuk was able to persuade the Mackenzie Inuit to let Franklin's party escape unharmed. By the end of the second expedition, Franklin had mapped out half of the Arctic seaboard.

In 1845 Franklin set sail with the ships *Erebus* and *Terror* to try to navigate the Northwest Passage. He planned to sail south from Lancaster Sound through Peel Sound and Franklin Strait. Just northwest of King William Island, Franklin's ships were frozen in by an ice jam. For eighteen long months the men held out in the ships, then they abandoned them and tried to make it back to the mainland. They never arrived. Between 1848 and 1854, nearly 150 British and American expeditions were organized to search for Franklin's men among the cluster of islands where they had disappeared. Local Inuit salvaged materials from the abandoned ships to turn into *snow knives* (for cutting snow) and other traditional tools. Franklin's men were never found alive, and it is thought that they died of

This engraving shows the American search expedition for the explorer Sir John Franklin and his men, who disappeared in 1845 among the frozen islands of the northern Arctic.

starvation. Although the search parties failed in their main goal, they did expand what Europeans knew about the Arctic, opening the way for ever more ambitious explorations.

FAMINE AND DISEASE ▪ By the mid-1800s, the booming trading, fishing, and whaling industries had wiped out much of the game on which the traders, fishermen, and whalers depended. Between 1800 and 1850, seals, salmon, bears, and walruses grew scarce. Hunters equipped with rifles were so efficient that they became wasteful and greedy, and some began shooting caribou for sinew alone. By the 1860s, whales were few and far between, and whalers started killing walruses for oil and ivory. Other whalers turned to trapping fox with steel traps. Hoping to find fresh supplies of wildlife, the traders spread farther north and west. By now, few Inuit could go back to their old self-sufficient ways, even if they had wanted to. Many had grown so used to their rifles that they had forgotten how to hunt with harpoons and knives. The tea, flour, woolen clothing, and tobacco that the Europeans gave them had become necessities. Although there were still some Inuit in the central Arctic who had never seen a European, European goods had become essential to the lives of most Inuit.

But the traders, whalers, and explorers introduced something else to the Arctic besides nice goods: They also brought with them horrible diseases that devastated the Inuit. Native peoples had no resistance against the illnesses carried by the Europeans. Smallpox, influenza, scarlet fever, and measles destroyed whole groups of Inuit all across the Arctic. By 1780, smallpox had spread far beyond the trading posts. In 1865 alone, three quarters of the Anderson River Inuit died of scarlet fever, and the Birch Creek Inuit were virtually killed off by the disease. An epidemic of measles and influenza from 1900 to 1902 took the lives of hundreds of Mackenzie Inuit in the Canadian Arctic. By 1910 only 130 people were left out of a population that had once numbered 2,000. Epidemics continued to destroy huge numbers of Inuit well into the twentieth century.

CHANGES IN ALASKA ▪ In 1867, the United States purchased Alaska from Russia. Although the fur trade was now in the hands of the United States, this did not alter the basic relationship between traders and the Inuit: The Inuit worked for the traders who controlled the flow of goods and supplies in the region. Toward the end of the century, when the demand for baleen whales from Alaska decreased, whalers began to establish themselves as traders in the settlements of northwest Alaska.

During this period, commercial salmon fishing and gold mining changed the nature of Inuit life in Alaska forever. Although the salmon industry that grew up around Bristol Bay in southwestern Alaska did not actually employ many native Inuit, the large numbers of outsiders who came to work in the canneries brought vast changes in the population and patterns of life in the area. In the same way, the Americans and Europeans who traveled along the Yukon River looking for gold were the first foreigners with whom the local Inuit were to have extensive contact.

MORE CHANGES ▪ After the decline of whaling, the Inuit communities in the central and northern Arctic were mainly managed by three groups: traders, missionaries, and the Canadian police. At the same time, the Canadian government, which had become independent from Britain in 1867, was beginning to extend its control.

In the early 1900s, there were trading posts throughout Inuit territory, and the government-run Hudson's Bay Company controlled nearly every one. Unlike the whalers, who never stayed long, the traders had an ongoing interest in the Inuit communities they dealt with, and they wanted the Inuit

This photograph shows children arriving for school in reindeer-drawn sleds. Actually, reindeer were a common sight throughout Alaska thirty years before the Hudson's Bay Company brought them into Canada.

to survive. In the 1920s, the Company imported reindeer from Norway in a plan to train the Inuit as herders. The Inuit in Alaska as well as Canada participated in this program. However, the plan failed, since the poorly trained Inuit were unsuccessful as herders. The traders also tried to move Inuit families to new hunting and trapping grounds, but the strange surroundings and separation from relatives made these relocations difficult. During hard times the traders gave bacon, flour, beans, and other food to the Inuit to tide them over. In the hungry winter of 1934, a local trading post manager sent out a sled to rescue nine starving Inuit. Sixteen others had died of hunger, he later reported.

Anglican and Roman Catholic missionaries opened schools and medical clinics for the Inuit. Until 1945, when the Canadian government became more actively involved, the missionaries were basically in charge of education and health in the Canadian Arctic.

By the early 1900s, the Royal North West Mounted Police (now the Royal Canadian Mounted Police) were in force throughout the four western provinces as well as northern Canada. Established to assert Canadian rule, their job was to keep order among the rough miners and gold rushers, the whalers, trappers, traders, explorers, Inuit, and Indians all mixed together in frontier towns. This was a hard change for the Inuit, who had been used to arranging their own system of law and justice. The Canadian government and the Inuit still struggle with the problem of how to apply Canadian law to the Inuit.

Chapter Five

THE INUIT TODAY

The 1940s and 1950s brought great changes to the Inuit. During World War II, many Inuit went to work at air bases and weather stations that were part of the North American defense system. Airlines, oil rigs, dams, roads, and mines reached well into the Arctic territory. At the same time, the collapse of fur prices in the 1940s and changes in the patterns of caribou migration in the 1950s sped up the movement away from traditional ways of living. More and more, Inuit families clustered into permanent towns, where they developed new ways of supporting themselves. Many Inuit formed cooperatives to share in hunting, fishing, and building, and making handicrafts and clothing.

INUIT ART ▪ Today, the Inuit are especially noted as artists and craftsmen, and their work is admired throughout the world. This is due largely to the inspiration and energy of James A. Houston, a Toronto native. As a young artist in 1949, Houston encouraged the Inuit to use their art as a way to earn money and improve their standard of living. Inuit soapstone and ivory carvings were the first works to be sold in the south.

Inuit children clown for the camera, using "sign language" familiar to kids the world over.

The Inuit also became skilled printmakers, usually depicting traditional scenes of nature. In this way, the Inuit express their deep attachment to their ancient culture.

"OUR LAND" ▪ Recently, the Inuit have begun to claim more control over their political and legal concerns. In 1971, the Alaska Native Claims Settlement Act (ANCSA) gave 44 million acres (almost 18 million hectares) of land and $962.5 million in cash to Alaska Natives, including American Indians and Inuit. The ANCSA divided Alaska into twelve Native regions, of which eight belong to the Aleut or Inuit. The Inuit developed local corporations to administer the land and cash. They invested in successful oil field businesses, mining operations, hotels, shipping companies, and even stocks and bonds.

In Canada, the Committee for Original Peoples Entitlement was formed in 1970 to represent the interests of the Inuit and other Native peoples in the Canadian government. During the decade that followed, several significant Inuit political organizations gained power. In 1982, Canada officially recognized a separate part of the Northwest Territories as belonging to the Inuit. This section is called *Nunavut*, meaning "Our Land," and it is governed by institutions that are controlled by the Inuit.

Today, there are about 42,000 Inuit and Aleut living in Alaska and an estimated 25,000 Inuit in Canada. Most Inuit live in conventional houses, shop for food, clothing, and supplies in stores, watch television, and drive snowmobiles. But technology cannot control the weather. The Inuit are still the people of a frozen land.

AN INUIT STORY:
HOW RAVEN BECAME BLACK

This is a story told by the Tikigaq people, the Inuit who live in north Alaska at the northwesternmost point in North America. The raven is a trickster figure.

■ ■ ■

Long ago, when animals were people, Raven and Loon were partners. They agreed to tattoo each other. "Me first," said Raven. (He was white at the beginning.) So Raven took lamp soot and drew little fire sparks on his partner's feathers. That was how Loon got the pattern on his feathers.

But Raven tired of painting. He grabbed some soot and ashes and tossed them over Loon's back. That's why it's gray now.

Loon was angry. He scooped soot from a pot and threw it at Raven.

Raven had been white. Now he's black. He stayed that way. There's no more to this story.

IMPORTANT
DATES

Circa 3000 B.C. Inuit ancestors migrate from Siberia to North America.

1500s   European explorers begin arriving on North American coast.

1670   Hudson's Bay Company founded.

1700   Thule culture becomes known as Inuit culture.

1700s   Russian explorers reach Alaskan coast to help establish fur trade.

1750s–1770s   German missionaries begin building stations along coastal regions in southwestern Alaska and Labrador, Newfoundland.

1780–1850   Main period of English, Scottish, and American Arctic exploration.

1800–1850   New England whalers dominate whale trade.

1819–1845   Captain John Franklin leads three Arctic expeditions, disappearing during final voyage.

1867   United States purchases Alaska from Russia.

1867	Canada gains independence from Great Britain.
1870s–1945	Inuit communities undergo rapid changes as miners, traders, missionaries, and Canadian mounted police basically take over their management.
1940s	Collapse of fur trade and opening up of Arctic to industrial production.
1950s	Formation of Inuit cooperatives.
1970s	Inuit in Alaska and Canada are granted land and political autonomy by governments of United States and Canada.

GLOSSARY

aglu. A breathing hole in sea ice used by seals.

amaut. A pouch for carrying a baby, sewn into the mother's coat.

angakok. A shaman, or a person with supernatural powers.

Arctic. The area in North America that lies closest to the North Pole; the area where the Inuit live.

Eskimo. Algonquian name for the Inuit, meaning "eaters of raw meat."

giviak. "Something dipped;" a festive dish served by the Inuit.

igloo. An Inuit house.

igluviaks. Snowhouses.

Inuit. The Inuit's name for themselves, meaning "the people."

kamik. Sealskin boots worn by the Inuit.

kashim. A big snowhouse used for communal gatherings.

kudlik. A stone lamp.

narwhal. Spotted whale, an Inuit delicacy; sinew used for sewing.

Nunavut. "Our Land," self-governed Inuit area in Canadian Northwest Territories.

snow knives. Knives used to cut ice and snow and build igluviaks.

taboo. A forbidden act, thing, or person.

tilugtut. A small saber of wood or bone, used to beat snow crystals from clothes before entering a house.

tundra. Windswept, snowy land.

ulo. A crescent-shaped bone knife, used to scrape and cut skins for clothing.

umiak. An open skin boat used in whale hunting, along with the kayak.

unaak. A harpoon used for hunting seals at breathing holes in sea ice.

wintering. Practice of nineteenth-century whalers of spending winters living ashore in huts among the Inuit until spring.

BIBLIOGRAPHY

*for children

Bruemmer, Fred. *Arctic Memories: Living with the Inuit.* Toronto: Key Porter Books, 1993.

Crowe, Keith J. *A History of the Original Peoples of Northern Canada.* Montreal: Queen's University Press, 1974.

Damas, David, vol. ed. *Handbook of North American Indians.* Vol. 5. Washington, D.C.: Smithsonian Institution, 1984.

Eber, Dorothy Harley. *When the Whalers Were Up North: Inuit Memories from the Eastern Arctic.* Boston: David R. Godine, 1989.

Freuchen, Peter. *Book of the Eskimos.* New York: Fawcett World Library, 1961.

Lowenstein, Tom. *Ancient Land, Sacred Whale: The Inuit Hunt and Its Rituals.* London: Bloomsbury, 1993.

———. *The Things That Were Said of Them: Shaman Stories and Oral Histories of the Tikigaq People.* Berkeley: University of California Press, 1992.

Merkur, Daniel. *Powers Which We Do Not Know: The Gods and Spirits of the Inuit.* Moscow: University of Idaho Press, 1991.

Nelson, Richard K. *Hunters of the Northern Ice.* Chicago: University of Chicago Press, 1969.

People of the Ice and Snow. Alexandria, Va.: Time-Life Books, 1994.

Purich, Donald. *The Inuit and Their Land: The Story of Nunavut.* Toronto: James Lorimer, 1992.

Rasmussen, Kund. *Across Arctic America: Narrative of the Fifth Thule Expedition.* New York: G.P. Putnam's Sons, 1927.

*———. Beyond the High Hills: A Book of Eskimo Poems. Cleveland: World Publishing, 1961.

*Shemic, Bonnie. *Houses of Snow, Skin and Bones: Native Dwellings of the Far North.* Montreal: Tundra Books, 1989.

*Siska, Heather Smith. *People of the Ice: How the Inuit Lived.* Vancouver, Canada: Douglas & McIntyre, 1980.

INDEX